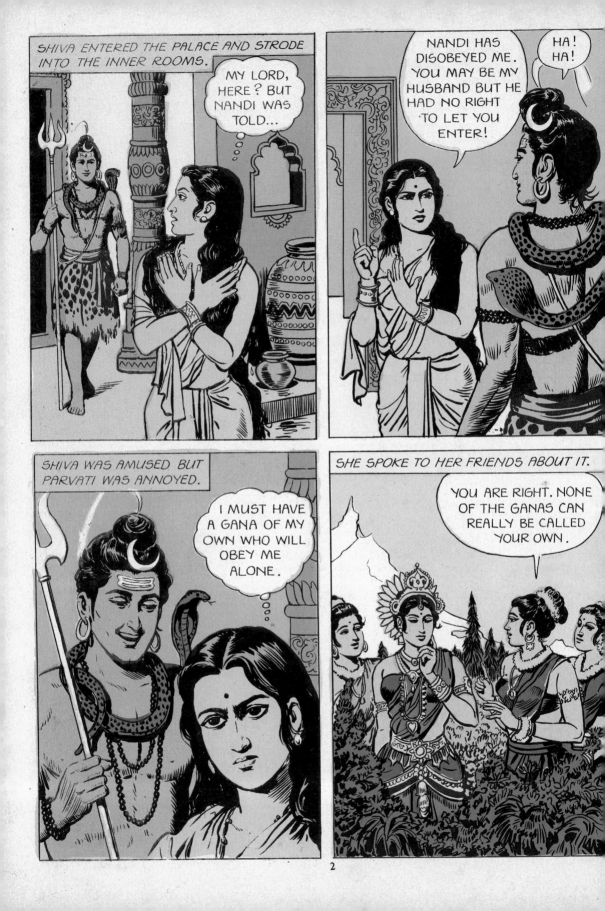

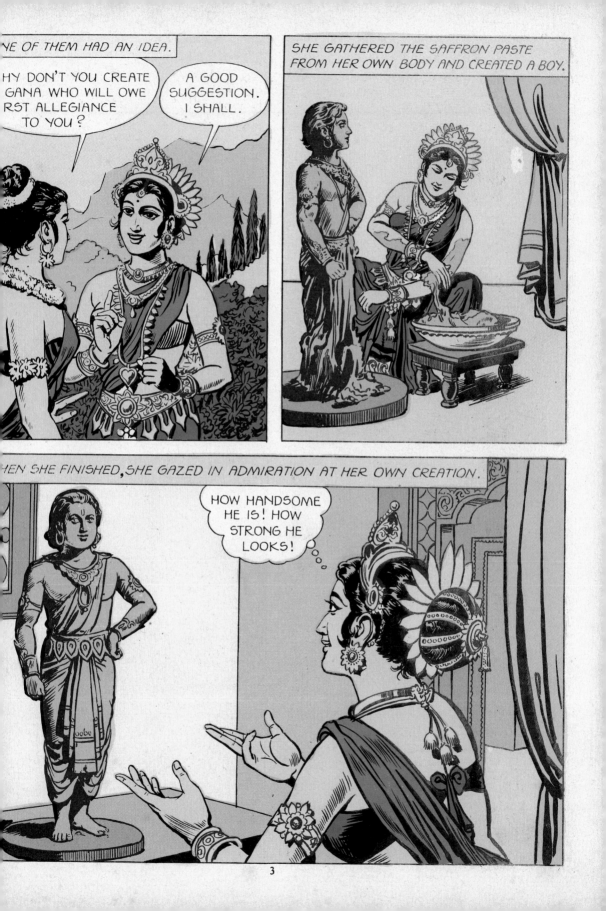

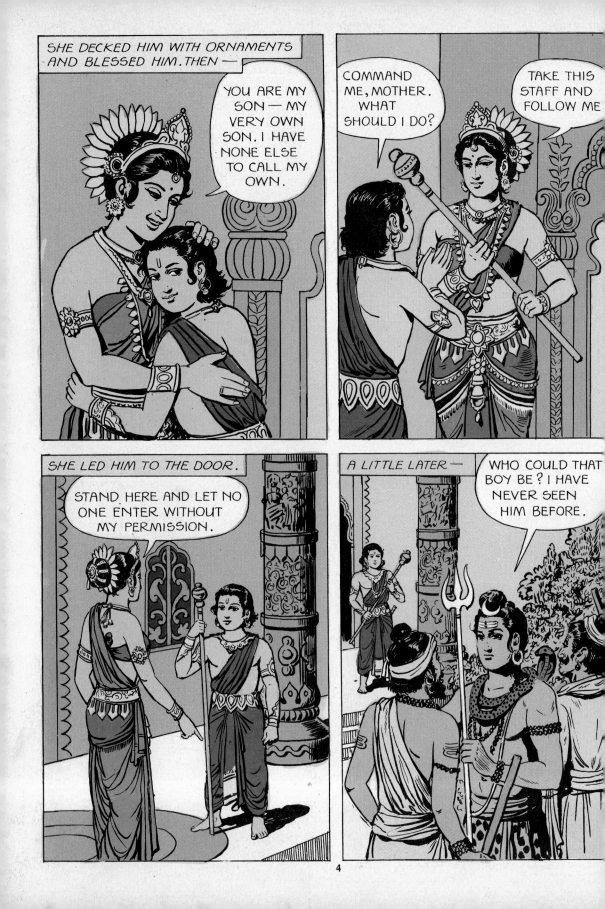

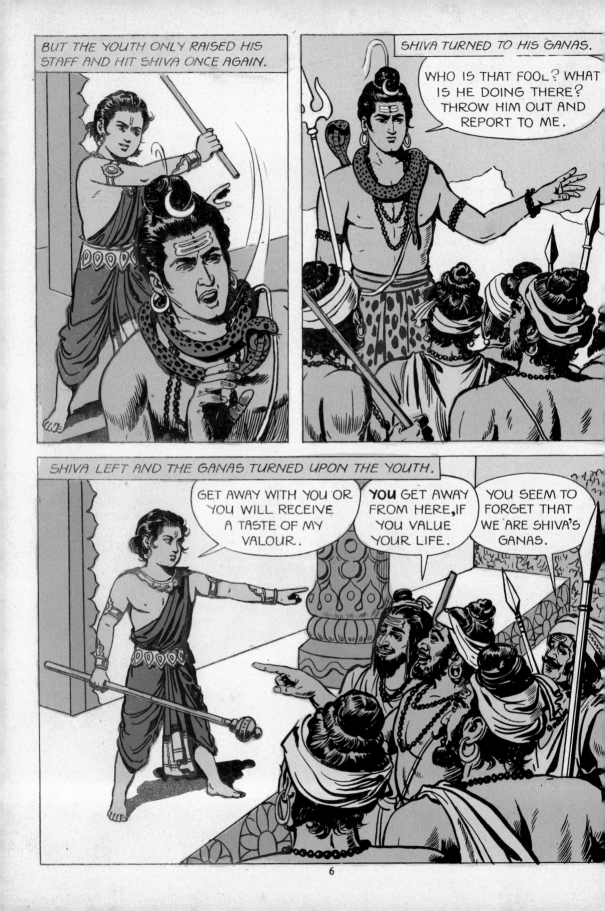

BUT WHY DID HE TRY TO FORCE HIS WAY IN? LET WHAT HAS TO HAPPEN, HAPPEN.

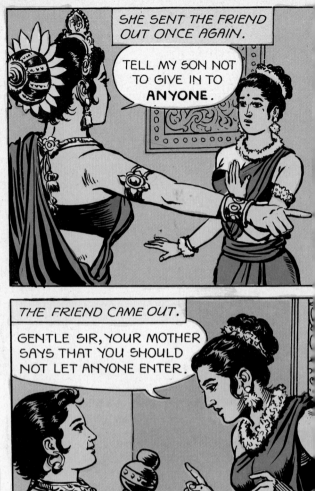

SHE SENT THE FRIEND OUT ONCE AGAIN.

TELL MY SON NOT TO GIVE IN TO **ANYONE.**

THE FRIEND CAME OUT.

GENTLE SIR, YOUR MOTHER SAYS THAT YOU SHOULD NOT LET ANYONE ENTER.

THE BOY WAS NO LONGER IN DOUBT. HE TURNED TO THE GANAS.

I AM THE SON OF PARVATI. YOU ARE THE GANAS OF SHIVA. YOU MUST CARRY OUT HIS ORDERS AND I — HERS.

8

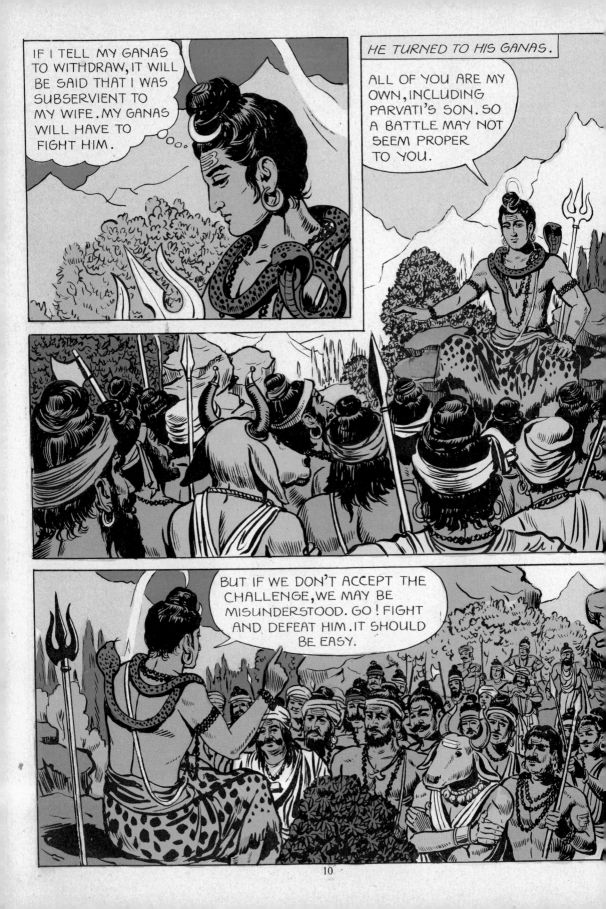

IF I TELL MY GANAS TO WITHDRAW, IT WILL BE SAID THAT I WAS SUBSERVIENT TO MY WIFE. MY GANAS WILL HAVE TO FIGHT HIM.

HE TURNED TO HIS GANAS.

ALL OF YOU ARE MY OWN, INCLUDING PARVATI'S SON. SO A BATTLE MAY NOT SEEM PROPER TO YOU.

BUT IF WE DON'T ACCEPT THE CHALLENGE, WE MAY BE MISUNDERSTOOD. GO! FIGHT AND DEFEAT HIM. IT SHOULD BE EASY.

MANY OF THE GANAS FELL.

THE REST FLED AS FAST AS THEY COULD.

THE BOY ONCE AGAIN TOOK HIS POST AT THE DOOR.

MEANWHILE, WHEN BRAHMA, VISHNU AND INDRA HEARD THE UPROAR, THEY TALKED THE MATTER OVER WITH SAGE NARADA.

GO TO LORD SHIVA. HE MAY NEED YOU.

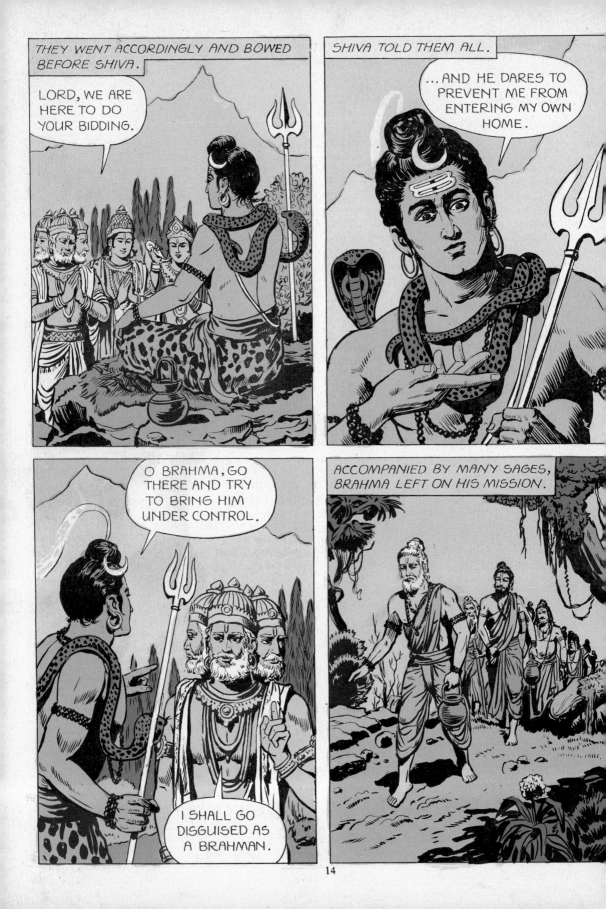

THEY WENT ACCORDINGLY AND BOWED BEFORE SHIVA.

LORD, WE ARE HERE TO DO YOUR BIDDING.

SHIVA TOLD THEM ALL.

...AND HE DARES TO PREVENT ME FROM ENTERING MY OWN HOME.

O BRAHMA, GO THERE AND TRY TO BRING HIM UNDER CONTROL.

I SHALL GO DISGUISED AS A BRAHMAN.

ACCOMPANIED BY MANY SAGES, BRAHMA LEFT ON HIS MISSION.

AS THEY NEARED HIM, THE YOUTH SUDDENLY JUMPED FORWARD AND—

THAT SHOULD TEACH YOU A LESSON.

BRAHMA WAS TAKEN UNAWARES.

I HAVE NOT COME TO FIGHT. I HAVE COME TO MAKE PEACE. LISTEN TO ME!

FOR AN ANSWER, THE YOUTH LIFTED HIS CLUB MENACINGLY.

DURGA TOOK THE FORM OF LIGHTNING...

...AND DESTROYED THE ENEMIES' WEAPONS BEFORE THEY COULD REACH THE BOY.

BETWEEN THE TWO OF THEM THEY DID NOT LET A SINGLE WEAPON COME ANYWHERE NEAR THE BOY'S SWINGING CLUB.

19

INDRA AND HIS DEVAS WERE COMPLETELY ROUTED.

EVEN KARTIKEYA, WHO HAD KILLED THE INVINCIBLE TARAKASURA, WAS HELPLESS.

THEY HELD COUNCIL.

WHAT SHOULD WE DO?

LET US GO BACK TO SHIVA.

UNPERTURBED BY THE SIGHT OF SHIVA, THE BOY ATTACKED! ALL THE CHIEF GODS. ONE BY ONE THEY FELL.

AS SHIVA WATCHED HIM FIGHT, HE WAS AMAZED.

HE IS INVINCIBLE. HE CAN ONLY BE KILLED BY CUNNING. I MUST WATCH FOR AN OPPORTUNITY.

THE SAME THOUGHT HAD STRUCK VISHNU TOO. HE SPOKE TO SHIVA.

I SHALL USE MY POWERS OF DELUSION TO FIGHT HIM, IF YOU PERMIT ME.

YOU MAY. THAT IS THE ONLY WAY.

BUT KALI AND DURGA DIVINED THEIR INTENTIONS.

WHAT SHOULD WE DO?

LET US CONFER ALL OUR STRENGTH ON THE YOUTH. THEN EVEN VISHNU'S MAYA WILL PROVE INEFFECTUAL.

WITH THE ADDED STRENGTH OF THE TWO SHAKTIS, THE BOY SWUNG HIS CLUB AT VISHNU.

VISHNU HAD TO USE ALL HIS ENERGY TO DODGE IT.

SHIVA SAW HIS PLIGHT AND CHARGED WITH HIS TRIDENT.

THE BOY LIFTED HIS CLUB...

...BUT IT WAS CUT IN TWO BY VISHNU'S DISCUS.

THE BOY HURLED THE PIECE THAT WAS LEFT IN HIS HAND...

.. BUT VISHNU'S MOUNT, GARUDA, CAUGHT IT AND PROTECTED HIS MASTER.

THEN, AS THE BOY PICKED UP HIS STAFF TO HIT VISHNU, SHIVA CAME UP FROM BEHIND AND...

...CUT OFF HIS HEAD.

FOR A MOMENT ALL ON THE SCENE STOOD STILL, THEIR GAZE FIXED ON THE VALIANT HERO.

THEN THE DEVAS AND THE GANAS BECAME JUBILANT.

BUT SHIVA WAS TROUBLED.

ALAS! WHAT HAVE I DONE? HOW SHALL I FACE PARVATI? HE WAS CREATED BY HER. THAT MADE HIM MY SON TOO.

MEANWHILE, WHEN PARVATI LEARNT OF HER SON'S DEATH—

MY SON WAS KILLED BY UNFAIR MEANS. FOR THIS THE DEVAS AND GANAS SHALL ALL DIE.

IT WAS A SINGLE-TUSKED ELEPHANT THAT MET THEM.

THEY BROUGHT THE HEAD BACK AND FITTED IT TO THE BODY OF THE BOY.

THE BOY SAT UP.

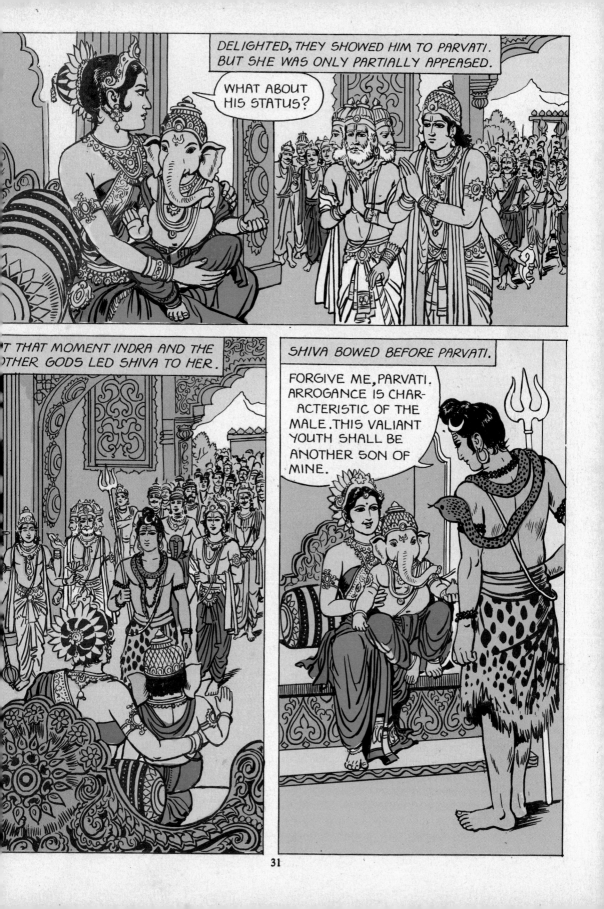

DELIGHTED, THEY SHOWED HIM TO PARVATI. BUT SHE WAS ONLY PARTIALLY APPEASED.

WHAT ABOUT HIS STATUS?

T THAT MOMENT INDRA AND THE OTHER GODS LED SHIVA TO HER.

SHIVA BOWED BEFORE PARVATI.

FORGIVE ME, PARVATI. ARROGANCE IS CHARACTERISTIC OF THE MALE. THIS VALIANT YOUTH SHALL BE ANOTHER SON OF MINE.

THEN SHIVA PLACED HIS HAND ON THE BOY'S HEAD.

EVEN AS A MERE BOY YOU SHOWED GREAT VALOUR. YOU SHALL BE GANESHA, THE PRESIDING OFFICER OF ALL MY GANAS. YOU SHALL BE WORTHY OF WORSHIP FOREVER. YOU SHALL ALSO BE CALLED VIGHNESHWARA, THE QUELLER OF OBSTACLES.

SHIVA AND PARVATI ONCE AGAIN BEGAN TO LIVE HAPPILY IN THEIR ABODE AT MOUNT KAILAS, DELIGHTED BY THE PRESENCE OF THEIR TWO SONS. TO THIS DAY, BEFORE ANY VENTURE IS UNDERTAKEN, IT IS GANESHA WHO IS INVOKED AND WHOSE BLESSINGS ARE SOUGHT.

HER MAGIC CHANGED THE PLACE INTO A PRETTY GARDEN WHERE SHE DANCED AND SANG MELODIOUSLY...

...TILL THE SAGE LOOKED UP.

PLEASE LET ME SERVE YOU AS YOUR WIFE, O HOLY ONE.

HOW CAN I REFUSE YOU, NOBLE MAIDEN!

SAGE KASHYAPA AND THE ASURA PRINCESS LIVED HAPPILY IN THE FOREST. IN DUE COURSE A SON WAS BORN TO THEM.

YOU, MY MIGHTY SURAPADMAN, SHALL BE THE LORD OF THE THREE WORLDS.

LATER MAYA GAVE BIRTH TO TWO MORE SONS WHOM SHE NAMED SIMHAMUKHA AND TARAKA.

I CAN'T WAIT FOR THE DAY WHEN YOU WILL CONQUER THE DEVAS AND MAKE THEM OUR SLAVES.

THE VIRTUOUS SAGE OF COURSE WAS IGNORANT OF MAYA'S DESIGNS

SO WHEN THE BOYS CAME OF AGE —

I AM GOING AWAY, MY SONS. TAKE CARE OF YOUR MOTHER, LEAD A VIRTUOUS LIFE AND BE DEVOTED TO THE LORD.

NOW IS THE TIME TO ACT. PROPITIATE LORD SHIVA AND OBTAIN BOONS WHICH WILL MAKE YOU INVINCIBLE.

AS YOU WISH, MOTHER.

THE THREE LEFT HOME AND PERFORMED SEVERE PENANCES TO WIN THE GRACE OF SHIVA.

BUT THEIR EFFORTS DID NOT BEAR FRUIT. SO SURAPADMAN, THE ELDEST, JUMPED INTO THE SACRIFICIAL FIRE.

BUT THE NEXT MOMENT HE WAS SAVED FROM ITS FLAMES BY SHIVA HIMSELF.

WHY ARE YOU SACRIFICING YOURSELF?

LORD, I WANT TO BE THE MASTER OF THE UNIVERSE. I WANT TO HAVE A BODY THAT WILL NOT PERISH.

NO ONE CAN HAVE AN IMMORTAL BODY. BUT YOU WILL BE INVINCIBLE AND RULE THE UNIVERSE FOR A LONG TIME TO COME.

YOU SHALL NOT BE DEFEATED BY ANY POWER EXCEPT MINE.

INTOXICATED WITH TRIUMPH, THE THREE BROTHERS RETURNED HOME AND TOLD HEIR MOTHER ABOUT SHIVA'S BOON.

AT LAST MY DREAM WILL COME TRUE.

YES, WE DON'T HAVE TO FEAR ANYONE. WE'LL SOON DRIV THE DEVAS OUT OF HEAVEN.

THEN, RAVAGING KINGDOM AFTER KINGDOM ON THEIR ROUTE···

...THEY CAME TO DEVALOKA. THERE, IN THE FIERCE BATTLE THAT FOLLOWED, THE DEVAS WERE ROUTED...

...AND TAKEN CAPTIVE.

ATER—

HA! HA! HOW DOES IT FEEL TO BE IN BONDAGE, INDRA, KING OF THE DEVAS?

IS THAT VAYU? HOW DEFLATED HE LOOKS!

HAT SHOULD WE O WITH THEM, BROTHER?

WE'LL MAKE THEM OUR SLAVES. INDRA WILL BE OUR FISHERMAN, AND VAYU OUR SWEEPER. AND...

...SURYA WILL MAKE A FINE BALL FOR OUR CHILDREN.

A BRILLIANT IDEA! HAHAHA!

SURAPADMAN HAD A MAGNIFICENT CITY BUILT BY VISHWAKARMA, THE ARCHITECT OF THE DEVAS. HE CALLED IT MAHENDRAPURI AND MADE IT HIS CAPITAL.

THE DEVAS MEANWHILE WERE LAMENTING THEIR FATE.

THEY HAVE IMPRISONED EVEN THE VALIANT JAYANTA*! WHAT SHALL WE DO?

HOW LONG CAN WE SUFFER THIS HUMILIATION?

SHIVA HAD PROMISED TO HELP US.

THAT WAS LONG AGO.

* INDRA'S SON

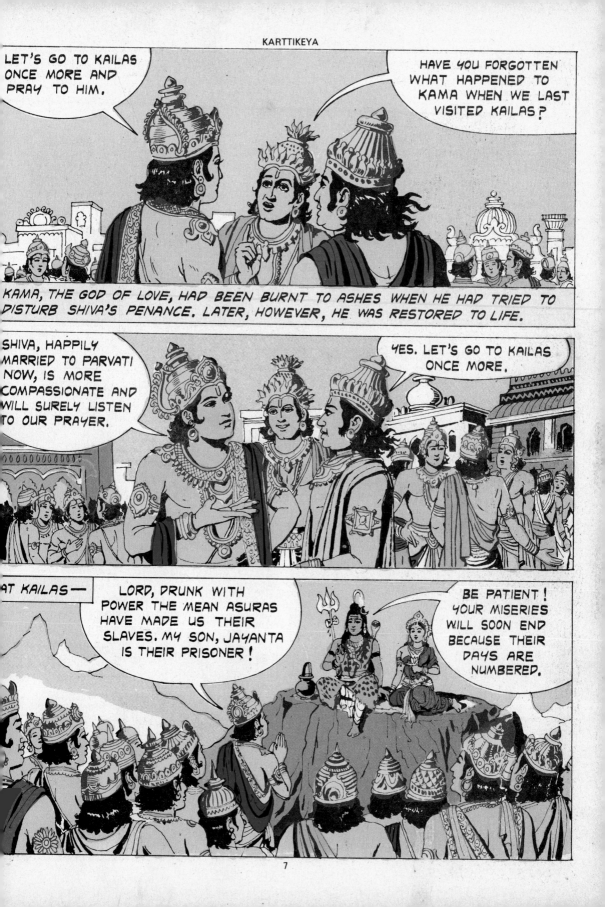

LET'S GO TO KAILAS ONCE MORE AND PRAY TO HIM.

HAVE YOU FORGOTTEN WHAT HAPPENED TO KAMA WHEN WE LAST VISITED KAILAS?

KAMA, THE GOD OF LOVE, HAD BEEN BURNT TO ASHES WHEN HE HAD TRIED TO DISTURB SHIVA'S PENANCE. LATER, HOWEVER, HE WAS RESTORED TO LIFE.

SHIVA, HAPPILY MARRIED TO PARVATI NOW, IS MORE COMPASSIONATE AND WILL SURELY LISTEN TO OUR PRAYER.

YES. LET'S GO TO KAILAS ONCE MORE.

AT KAILAS—

LORD, DRUNK WITH POWER THE MEAN ASURAS HAVE MADE US THEIR SLAVES. MY SON, JAYANTA IS THEIR PRISONER!

BE PATIENT! YOUR MISERIES WILL SOON END BECAUSE THEIR DAYS ARE NUMBERED.

THEN SHIVA ASSUMED A FORM WITH SIX FACES...

...FROM WHICH SIX DIVINE SPARKS SHOT FORTH...

...DAZZLING THE DEVAS WITH THEIR SPLENDOUR.

THE CHILD BORN OUT OF THESE SPARKS WILL SLAY THE ASURAS.

SHIVA THEN ASSUMED HIS ORIGINAL FORM.

VAYU, YOU AND AGNI CARRY THESE SPARKS TO GANGA. SHE'LL CARRY THEM TO THE SHARAVANA* ON THE UDAYA MOUNTAIN.

*FOREST OF REEDS

8

AGNI AND VAYU FLEW WITH THE SPARKS···

··· TO GANGA.

SHIVA HAS ASKED YOU TO CARRY THESE TO THE REED FOREST ON THE UDAYA MOUNTAIN.

AS SOON AS GANGA BROUGHT THEM INTO THE SHARAVANA···

··· THE SPARKS TURNED INTO SIX BABIES!

JUST THEN SIX CELESTIAL NYMPHS CALLED THE KRITTIKAS HAPPENED TO PASS BY.

NEWBORN BABIES! SIX OF THEM!

ONE FOR EACH OF US!

AND THE KRITTIKAS BEGAN TO CUDDLE THE INFANTS.

THE DEVAS CAME ON THE SCENE A LITTLE LATER.

LOOK! THE CHILD...

YOU MEAN CHILDREN!

AND THEN CAME SHIVA AND PARVATI.

SHIVA'S CHILDREN! MY CHILDREN!

PEACE! PEACE! AS PARVATI'S SON HE WILL BE NAMED SKANDA AND AS THE SON OF THE GODDESS OF THE FOREST, SHARAVANA; AS THE KRITTIKAS' SON, KARTTIKEYA AND AS GANGA'S KUMARA; AS AGNI'S SON, MAHASENA AND AS MINE, GUHA.

HOW WILL I FONDLE A BABY WITH SIX HEADS?

THE NEXT MINUTE—

MY SON!

KARTTIKEYA WAS NOW LIKE ANY OTHER CHILD.

SOON, NINE DIVINE BEINGS EMERGED FROM THE LAKE.

THOSE ARE YOUR GANAS—VEERABAHU AND HIS COMPANIONS.

THEN, AFTER THE DEVAS HAD WORSHIPPED LORD KARTTIKEYA ...

...SHIVA TOOK HIM TO HIS OWN ABODE, AT MOUNT KAILASA.

ONE DAY AT KAILASA—

PARVATI, THE TIME HAS COME FOR KARTTIKEYA TO SUBDUE TARAKASURA, SIMHAMUKHA, AND SURAPADMAN.

BUT HE IS JUST A CHILD, MY LORD, AND THEY ARE MIGHTY WARRIORS.

YES, BUT HE IS THE CHILD WITH THE DIVINE SPARK. BESIDES, HIS GANAS WILL GO WITH HIM.

SHIVA SUMMONED KARTTIKEYA AND VEERABAHU.

GET READY TO ATTACK SURAPADMAN AND HIS BROTHERS.

WHEN THE PREPARATIONS WERE COMPLETED—

YOU SHALL LEAD THE DEVAS TO VICTORY. CRUSH THE ASURAS AND LIBERATE THE DEVAS. HERE IS THE MATCHLESS VEL, YOUR SPEAR. MAY SUCCESS BE YOURS!

ARMED WITH THE SPEAR, KARTTIKEYA SET OUT IN PURSUIT OF THE ASURAS.

AFTER HE HAD COVERED SOME DISTANCE —

YOU WILL HAVE TO FACE ME, YOUNG BOY, BEFORE YOU PROCEED FURTHER.

IT WAS THE ASURA, KRAUNCHA IN THE FORM OF A MOUNTAIN.

WITHOUT A WORD, KARTTIKEYA HURLED HIS SPEAR...

...AND KRAUNCHA WAS NO MORE.

14

16

THEN HE FLEW INTO SURAPADMAN'S COURT.

I WILL ASSUME MY OWN FORM NOW. WILL SURAPADMAN OFFER ME A SEAT?

THE NEXT MOMENT—

A THRONE FOR ME! IT MUST BE THE WORK OF LORD KARTTIKEYA!

WHO... WHO ARE YOU?

I AM LORD KARTTIKEYA'S MESSENGER.

KARTTIKEYA! THE BOY WHO SLEW MY BROTHER!

YES. LORD KARTTIKEYA WANTS YOU TO RELEASE JAYANTA AND STOP TORTURING THE DEVAS OR ELSE...

...YOU WILL MEET WITH THE SAME FATE AS YOUR BROTHER!

A MERE CHILD DARES THREATEN ME! I'LL I'LL...

WHERE HAS HE GONE?

HE...HE'S VANISHED!

THERE WAS AN UNEASY SILENCE FOR A MOMENT. THEN SIMHAMUKHA SPOKE.

MY INSTINCT TELLS ME THAT THIS KARTTIKEYA IS NO ORDINARY BOY.

MEANWHILE VEERABAHU HAD REACHED KARTTIKEYA'S CAMP.

IT'S NO USE. SURAPADMAN WANTED TO CAPTURE ME TOO!

WELL, WE'LL MEET THEM IN BATTLE. PREPARE TO MARCH TO MAHENDRAPURI.

WHEN KARTTIKEYA'S ARMY REACHED THE OUTSKIRTS OF MAHENDRAPURI, SURAPADMAN SENT HIS SON BANUKOPAN TO SUBDUE THEM.

BANUKOPAN FELL UPON THE DEVA ARMY.

ON THE SECOND DAY OF THE BATTLE—

COME, BANUKOPAN. TODAY, YOU SHALL NOT RETURN HOME.

I CERTAINLY WON'T. NOT TILL I'VE KILLED EVERY ONE OF YOU.

VEERABAHU RUSHED AT HIM AND THE TWO FOUGHT LONG AND HARD.

AT LAST BANUKOPAN FELL AND THE ASURAS FLED IN PANIC.

THE DEATH OF BANUKOPAN SHOOK SURAPADMAN.

SAVE US, SIMHAMUKHA!

I WILL DO MY BEST, BROTHER.

SO THE NEXT DAY SIMHAMUKHA LED THE ATTACK. THE ARMY OF THE DEVAS REELED UNDER HIS ONSLAUGHT.

THEN SIMHAMUKHA SENT A MISSILE···

···WHICH WOUND ITSELF AROUND VEERABAHU, HIS BROTHER AND THE REST OF THE ARMY···

··AND HURLED THEM···

···FAR, FAR AWAY FROM THE BATTLEFIELD.

BUT KARTTIKEYA MEANWHILE HAD SENT FORTH SEVERAL MISSILES TO COUNTER THE MOVE.

SOON—

THEN KARTTIKEYA TURNED HIS ATTENTION TO SIMHAMUKHA.

YOU SHOULD NOT MISUSE THE POWERS ACQUIRED BY YOU. YOU SHOULD...

HAVE YOU COME HERE TO FIGHT OR TO PREACH?

AFTER A FIERCE BATTLE KARTTIKEYA HURLED INDRAYUDHA* AT SIMHAMUKHA.

AS SIMHAMUKHA FELL—

YOUR WEAPON HAS SHATTERED MY EGO. NOW I SEE YOU IN ALL YOUR GLORY. O LORD, BLESS ME.

THE MERCIFUL KARTTIKEYA BLESSED SIMHAMUKHA.

YOU SHALL SERVE GODDESS KALI AS HER VEHICLE.

*INDRA'S WEAPON, THE THUNDERBOLT

SURAPADMAN QUICKLY ASSUMED THE FORM OF A HUGE BIRD...

...AND CHARGED AT KARTTIKEYA.

KARTTIKEYA HOWEVER USING INDRA IN THE FORM OF PEACOCK AS HIS MOUNT...

BUT SURAPADMAN ESCAPED IN THE NICK OF TIME BY TAKING THE FORM OF A TREE.

...LASHED OUT AT HIM.

AND—

A-A-H

AS HE FELL, A GREAT CHANGE CAME OVER SURAPADMAN.

LORD, PARDON ME. I REPENT FOR MY EVIL ACTS. LORD, I SEEK REFUGE IN YOU.

KARTTIKEYA LOOKED AT THE FALLEN ASURA WITH COMPASSION.

SURAPADMAN, REPENTANCE WASHES AWAY ALL ONE'S SINS. YOU SHALL SERVE ME AS MY VEHICLE AND ALSO AS MY EMBLEM.

THUS SURAPADMAN ASSUMED TWO FORMS—ONE OF A PEACOCK TO SERVE AS A VEHICLE TO THE LORD AND ANOTHER OF A COCK TO ADORN KARTTIKEYA'S FLAG POST.

O KARTTIKEYA, WE BOW TO YOU IN REVERENCE.

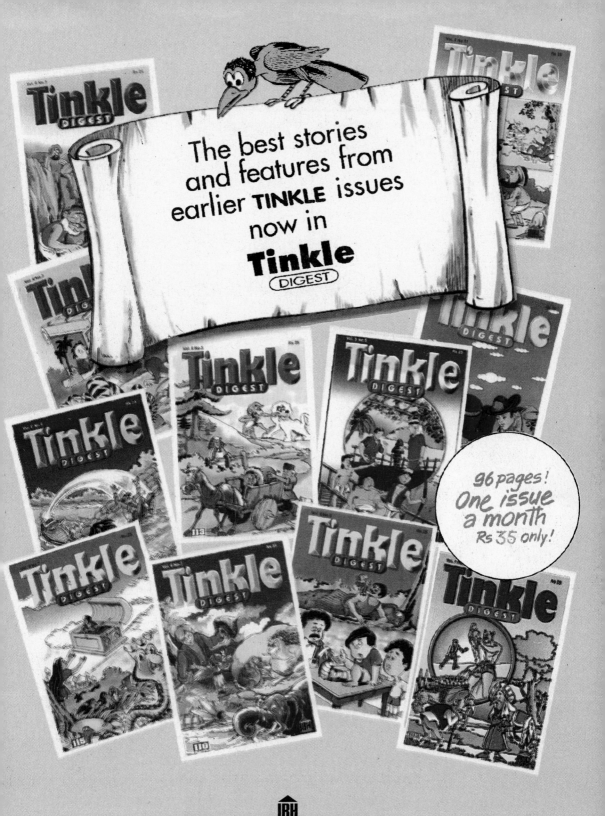

AYYAPPAN

KING RAJASHEKHARA, THE WEALTHY RULER OF PANTHALAM, IN KERALA, HAD NO CHILDREN.

HIS SUBJECTS WERE WORRIED.

IF THERE IS NO HEIR TO THE THRONE, WHAT WILL BECOME OF US WHEN OUR KING DIES?

O THAT HE WERE BLESSED WITH A SON.

YES. A SON AS PIOUS AND GENEROUS AS HE IS!

HIS AMBITIOUS DIWAN, HOWEVER, WAS HAPPY.

AS LONG AS THERE IS NO HEIR TO THE THRONE, WHEN RAJASHEKHARA DIES HIS KINGDOM WILL CERTAINLY BE MINE.

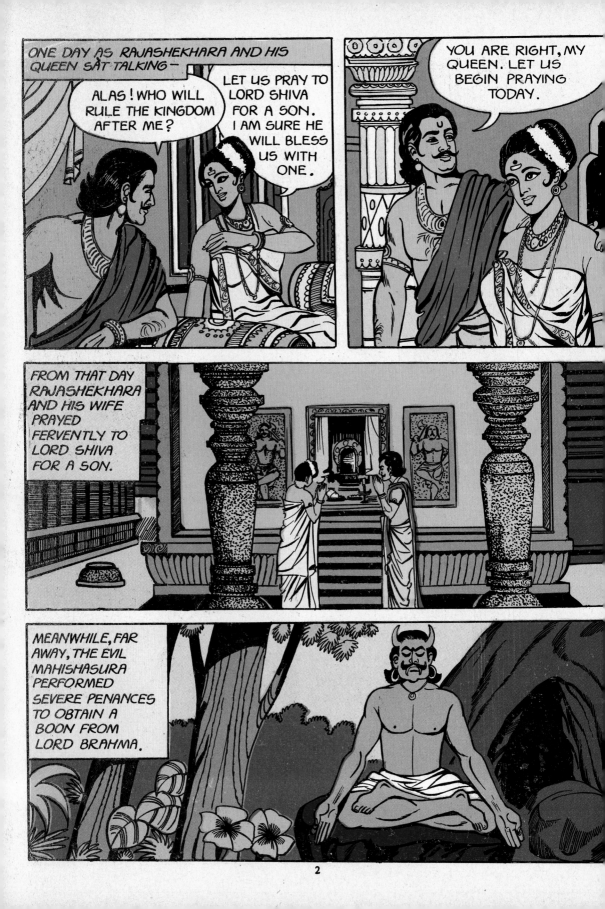

EMBOLDENED BY THE BOON, MAHISHASURA BEGAN HARASSING ALL ON EARTH.

THE EVIL ONE IS HERE!

O DEVAS, SAVE US!

RUN!

THE DEVAS HELD COUNCIL.

THIS ASURA MUST BE DESTROYED. BECAUSE OF BRAHMA'S BOON, ONLY A WOMAN WOULD BE ABLE TO DO IT.

THEN LET US EVOKE ONE WITH OUR COMBINED POWERS.

HER MISSION ACCOMPLISHED, CHANDIKA DEVI ASCENDED TO HEAVEN.

WHEN MAHISHI, THE WIFE OF MAHISHASURA, LEARNT OF HER HUSBAND'S DEATH—

I SHALL TEACH THE DEVAS A LESSON. IT WAS THEY WHO INVOKED THE DEVI.

MAHISHI UNDERTOOK A DEEP PENANCE TO PROPITIATE LORD BRAHMA. HE APPEARED BEFORE HER.

MAHISHI! WHAT DO YOU DESIRE?

THAT I SHOULD NOT MEET MY DEATH AT THE HANDS OF EITHER VISHNU OR SHIVA!

BRAHMA GRANTED HER THE BOON AND VANISHED.

8

9

AS SOON AS THE INFANT WAS CREATED—

I WILL TIE THIS GOLD BELL AROUND HIS NECK BEFORE I TAKE HIM TO EARTH.

MEANWHILE, ON EARTH, RAJASHEKHARA WAS OUT HUNTING WITH HIS RETINUE.

AFTER A TIRING DAY WHILE THE PARTY RELAXED ON THE BANKS OF THE RIVER PAMPA...

...RAJASHEKHARA WANDERED OFF ALONE.

HOW PEACEFUL AND QUIET IT IS HERE.

BY THE TIME MANIKANTHAN'S STUDIES WERE OVER, THE GURU KNEW THAT HE WAS A DIVINE CHILD.

SIR, PLEASE ACCEPT MY GURU-DAKSHINA.*

FROM YOU I WANT COMPASSION. NOT THESE.

THEN THE GURU BROUGHT HIS BLIND AND MUTE SON BEFORE MANIKANTHAN.

MANIKANTHAN, PLEASE RESTORE HIS SIGHT AND SPEECH.

MANIKANTHAN BLESSED THE BOY.

THEY ARE HIS.

THE GURU'S SON SAW LIGHT.

FATHER! I HAVE BEEN GIVEN A NEW LIFE!

AFTER THIS FIRST MIRACLE MANIKANTHAN PERFORMED MANY MORE. THE NEWS SPREAD.

I HAVE NEVER SEEN SUCH A GIFTED BOY.

OUR FUTURE IS ASSURED. HE WILL SUCCEED THE KING.

THE DIWAN, WHO OVERHEARD THESE COMMENTS...

*THE TRADITIONAL TRIBUTE GIVEN BY A DISCIPLE TO HIS TEACHER

16

THE QUEEN HAS A SEVERE HEADACHE. YOU WILL PRESCRIBE TIGRESS'S MILK AS THE ONLY REMEDY.

VERY WELL.

JUST THEN A MESSENGER CAME TO THE PHYSICIAN.

THE QUEEN IS IN AGONY. THE KING HAS ASKED YOU TO EXAMINE HER IMMEDIATELY.

AFTER THE PHYSICIAN HAD EXAMINED THE QUEEN—

WHAT IS THE QUICKEST REMEDY? I CAN-NOT BEAR TO SEE MY QUEEN IN PAIN.

THE ONLY REMEDY FOR THIS AILMENT IS TIGRESS'S MILK.

THEN, EXACTLY AS THE WICKED DIWAN HAD FORESEEN—

FATHER, LET ME GO ON THIS ERRAND!

MANIKANTHAN, NO! YOU ARE TOO YOUNG.

FOR MY MOTHER'S SAKE LET ME GO, FATHER.

HOW CAN I LET YOU GO ON SUCH A DANGEROUS VENTURE.

BUT MANIKANTHAN PERSISTED AND RAJASHEKHARA HAD TO YIELD.

ALL RIGHT, MY SON. GO IF YOU MUST. BUT TAKE CARE.

MANIKANTHAN SET OUT FOR THE FOREST.

AS HE WANDERED DEEPER AND DEEPER INTO IT HE CAME TO THE DOMAIN OF MAHISHI, WHO LIVED IN THAT FOREST.

WHO IS THIS CREATURE WHO DARES TO TRESPASS ON OUR FOREST? I MUST TELL MY MISTRESS.

THE ASURA RAN TO MAHISHI.

THERE IS A BOY ROAMING IN OUR FORESTS.

HOW DARE HE, WITHOUT MY PERMISSION! I'LL DESTROY HIM.

MAHISHI WENT UP TO MANIKANTHAN AND ATTACKED HIM.

COME, MAHISHI. MY EARTHLY MISSION IS ABOUT TO BE FULFILLED.

A FIERCE BATTLE ENSUED.

MANIKANTHAN SOON KILLED MAHISHI.

AS MANIKANTHAN CONTINUED HIS SEARCH FOR A TIGRESS, INDRA, KING OF THE DEVAS, APPEARED BEFORE HIM.

I SHALL TAKE THE FORM OF A TIGRESS AND COME WITH YOU INTO THE CITY AS YOUR MOUNT.

THE DEVAS WHO HAD ACCOMPANIED INDRA ALSO TURNED THEMSELVES INTO TIGRESSES.

WE WILL FOLLOW YOU INTO THE CITY.

AS MANIKANTHAN RODE INTO THE CITY ON HIS TERRIFYING MOUNT FOLLOWED BY AN EQUALLY TERRIFYING RETINUE—

TIGERS!'

HELP! RUN!

ONE OF THE CITIZENS RAN TO RAJASHEKHARA.

MANIKANTHAN HAS RETURNED... WITH A HORDE OF TIGRESSES.

THE KING, WHO RUSHED OUT TO SEE THIS UNUSUAL SIGHT, WAS STUNNED.

MANIKANTHAN IS TWELVE TODAY. TODAY I WILL KNOW WHO HE IS.

24

27

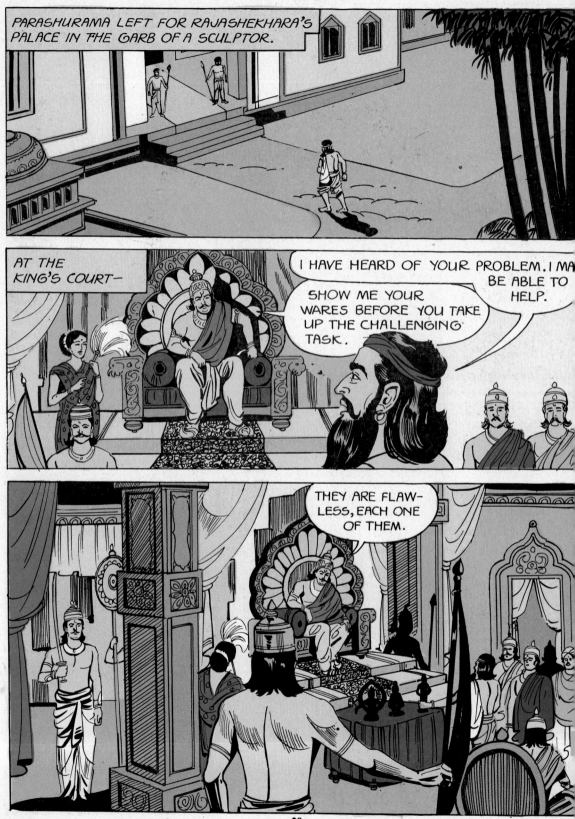

PARASHURAMA LEFT FOR RAJASHEKHARA'S PALACE IN THE GARB OF A SCULPTOR.

AT THE KING'S COURT—

I HAVE HEARD OF YOUR PROBLEM. I MA BE ABLE TO HELP.

SHOW ME YOUR WARES BEFORE YOU TAKE UP THE CHALLENGING TASK.

THEY ARE FLAW-LESS, EACH ONE OF THEM.

29

MEANWHILE THE WICKED DIWAN WAS AFFLICTED BY AN INCURABLE DISEASE.

I HAVE SINNED. WILL I EVER BE CLEANSED?

ONE NIGHT HE HAD A DREAM.

COME TO MY TEMPLE ON THE SHABARI HILL. BUT ENTER ONLY AFTER CLEANSING YOURSELF IN THE PAMPA.*

THE DIWAN WASTED NO TIME. THE NEXT MORNING HE SET OUT FOR THE PAMPA.

I HAVE COME TO WASH AWAY MY SINS IN REMORSE, HOLY MOTHER. SAVE ME.

THE DIWAN CAME OUT OF THE WATER GLOWING WITH HEALTH —

I AM CLEANSED. THE HOLY MOTHER HAS BEEN MERCIFUL.

* RIVER SAID TO BE ENLIVENED BY THE SPIRIT OF SHABARI, THE DEVOTEE OF LORD RAMA.